OUT AND ABOUT
NIGHT EXPLORER

A children's guide to over 100
insects, animals, birds and stars

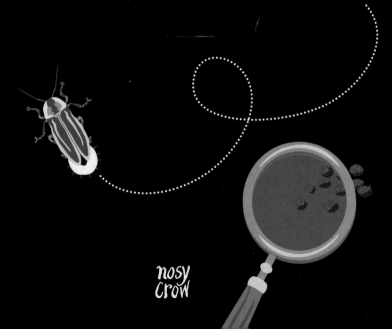

nosy
crow

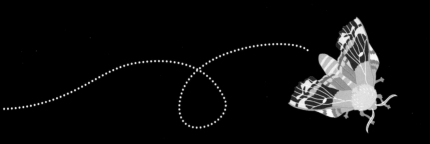

First published in the United Kingdom in 2017 by Nosy Crow Ltd
The Crow's Nest, 14 Baden Place, Crosby Row
London SE1 1YW
www.nosycrow.com

This edition published 2019

ISBN 978 1 78800 440 4

Printed in China
Papers used by Nosy Crow are made from wood grown in sustainable forests.

1 3 5 7 9 8 6 4 2

CONTENTS

INTRODUCTION

There's plenty of fun to be had outdoors – even when the sun has gone down! This book is packed full of fun activities and useful tips to help you explore nature at night.

You might wonder whether there's that much difference between nature during the daytime and by night. But, if you check out the wildlife at the end of each day, you'll find there's a strange and exciting night-time world out there.

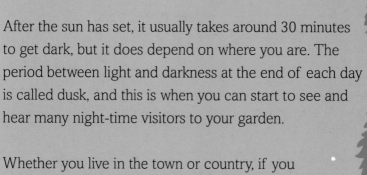

After the sun has set, it usually takes around 30 minutes to get dark, but it does depend on where you are. The period between light and darkness at the end of each day is called dusk, and this is when you can start to see and hear many night-time visitors to your garden.

Whether you live in the town or country, if you keep your eyes and ears open, there's plenty of nocturnal nature to be found . . .

READY TO EXPLORE

TOP 10 TIPS FOR SEEKING WILDLIFE

1 **Don't get lost.** Pay attention to the way you are walking. Take a map or a compass if you have one and check the route before you go out.

2 **Make a walking stick.** It's much more fun to go on a walk with a sturdy stick to help you.

3 **Be quiet.** Listen out and avoid wearing rustly clothes or speaking loudly. Try to watch out for things like dry twigs and crunchy leaves so you don't step on them and frighten away any animals.

4 **Avoid sudden bright lights.** They can frighten animals away, too.

5 **Look all around you.** Don't just look straight ahead: look behind you, look up in trees for silhouettes of animals against the sky, and look down on the ground.

6   **Do your research.** You need to know about the animals that you are tracking, what its tracks look like and how to follow them, and how the animal behaves in the wild.

7   **Set out to attract nocturnal animals.** See pages 24, 34 and 40 for ideas. Insects attract bats and small mammals, so if you attract them, you may start to see owls as well!

8   **Follow your nose.** If you can smell sweet flowers, then wild animals (especially moths) will be attracted to them.

9   **Leave wild animals alone.** Remember, it's always important to give wild animals space, day or night. Don't corner any animal or stick a torch or camera in their face. Even if an animal seems totally harmless, you should still keep your distance.

10   **Have fun!**

ALL RIGHT AT NIGHT

If it's your first time exploring wildlife at night or even if you go out every weekend, the most important thing to remember is to be prepared. Some people might think the dark is a bit scary, but there's no need to be scared if you're well prepared!

1 **Never go out alone at night.** If you're going beyond your own garden then always take a grown-up with you, as well as a charged mobile phone in case of emergencies. When you are out and about, don't wander off – always stay together with your group.

2 **Choose familiar territory.** Go to places that you have already visited during the daytime so that you know what the landscape looks like. Check a map first in the light and plan your route. This means you won't run into any surprises like steep drops or sudden ditches!

3 **Practise improving your night vision.** If you spend time in the dark before you head outside, your eyes will start to adjust and you will be able to see more without the help of a torch. Did you know that eating carrots helps to improve your night vision, too?

4 **Use a checklist to make sure you don't forget anything important.** You can have fun looking for wildlife in your garden with no equipment at all, but if you're planning to venture further away or even planning to stay outdoors overnight, then you should start to think about taking more equipment with you. Here are some ideas for useful things to take with you on your adventure:

TASTY SNACKS

MOBILE PHONE

DARK CLOTHES & GLOVES

HAT

WATERPROOF JACKET

STURDY SHOES OR WELLIES

NOTEBOOK & PENCIL

WATER

FIRST AID

SMALL FIRST AID KIT

MAKING A NIGHT-TIME DEN

You don't need to travel far and wide to find interesting nocturnal wildlife – your garden is a great place to start exploring! You can practise putting up your tent and sleeping outdoors in your own garden first (you won't have to go far if you've forgotten anything or if you need help), then you can move further away from home when you're ready – and your parents are, too! If you do start exploring away from home, make sure you don't go out alone.

What about making a secret outdoor den? You could build a den during the daytime and then visit it at night to spy on wildlife.

To make a teepee, you need to find five or six long sticks and tie them together at one end. Stand them up (with the tied end at the top) and pull the poles outwards to form a teepee shape. Push the poles into the ground and weave bendy branches between the poles to fill in the sides.

11

USING A TORCH

You don't have to use a torch all the time while you're outdoors, but it's best to have one with you just in case. Remember to check your batteries before you head out and always take a spare set. A wind-up torch can be useful because you never have to worry about the batteries dying. A head torch can be even more useful as you can light the way while still having both hands free. Wild animals are less bothered by red light, so you could try fixing some red cellophane (or a red sweet wrapper!) over the beam of your torch using elastic bands or sticky tape.

You can also use your torch to send Morse Code signals. 'Save Our Ship' in Morse code means 'help'. In an emergency, to signal SOS flash three short flashes, then three long ones, and end with three more short flashes. For fun, you could try signalling your name!

A	●—	J	●———	S	●●●
B	—●●●	K	—●—	T	—
C	—●—●	L	●—●●	U	●●—
D	—●●	M	——	V	●●●—
E	●	N	—●	W	●——
F	●●—●	O	———	X	—●●—
G	——●	P	●——●	Y	—●——
H	●●●●	Q	——●—	Z	——●●
I	●●	R	●—●		

Torches can be fun too and you can use them to play a game of tag! To play, you will need at least three friends and a safe space to run around in. The more places to hide, the more exciting the game will be!

1 Everyone has one minute to run and hide with their switched-off torches.

2 Being careful not to be seen in the dark, each player then starts to search for their friends.

3 A player is out if someone sneaks up and flashes their torch on them.

4 Keep playing until there is only one player left – they are the winner!

1 ●—————		6 —●●●●	
2 ●●————		7 ——●●●	
3 ●●●———		8 ———●●	
4 ●●●●—		9 ————●	
5 ●●●●●		10 —————	

SHADOW-PUPPET THEATRE

Even inside a tent, you can still have fun – all you need is a torch and your hands! Set up the torch so that it shines onto the wall of the tent, hold your hands in front of the torch (about 60 cm away) and try making interesting shadow shapes which will appear on the wall. Here are a few ideas to get you started, then try making up some animals of your own!

bull

wolf

 rabbit

elephant

 fox

15

ANIMALS

HEDGEHOG PRINTS

LOOKING FOR CLUES

It can be really tricky to spot animals at night, but even the stealthiest creatures sometimes leave clues.

Animal tracks

Look for footprints while you're out exploring – they might just lead you to an animal! Count the number of toes and claws on any tracks you find. This will help you decide what type of animal you are following.

Badger pawprints are large and they have five toes with long claws.

BADGER PRINTS

A fox pawprint has the same number of pads as a dog's pawprint, but the foot shape is slightly narrower.

FOX PRINTS

16

Hedgehog footprints are tough to spot because they are so small, but they are also very distinctive. They have three toes that point forward and two that go out to the sides!

Rabbit tracks are some of the easiest to identify because their back paws leave much deeper prints than their front paws.

RABBIT PRINTS

The best place to find footprints is on a thin layer of snow or on soft ground. It's very rare to find clear prints – often you'll just find part of a pawprint – and the quality depends on how fast the animal has been moving.

DEER PRINTS

Some animals walk the same route every day, so a path gets marked on the ground. Badgers go in and out of their sett fairly regularly, so you'll find deep tracks leading to the entrance and it will mostly be clear of leaves.

BIRD PRINTS

17

LOOKING FOR CLUES

Trails of scent

Some animals leave a trail that you can smell – foxes and grass snakes both leave strong, sharp smells!

Scent-marking is an important part of communication between some nocturnal animals, as visual signals cannot easily be seen in the dark. They use powerful smells to mark trees and the ground to show the boundaries of their territory – or to attract a mate.

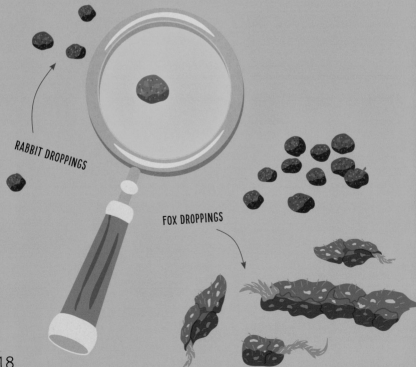

RABBIT DROPPINGS

FOX DROPPINGS

Animal poo

Keep an eye out for poo, too! If you find any droppings, there might be an animal nearby. Some mammals use their poo as a way of marking their territories so you can often find it in quite obvious places. Always remember to look – but don't touch!

Badgers always poo in the same place – they have family toilets called latrines, so if you find a big pile of badger poo, there must be a sett nearby! Often they smell sweet and musky. Their poo looks different depending on what they have eaten – soft and runny if they've had worms for dinner, but firm like a sausage with seeds inside if they've eaten fruit or wheat.

Rabbit and hare pellets are made up of finely-chewed grass. It can be difficult to tell the droppings apart but hare pellets are a little bit larger and more flattened. Like badgers, you'll often find piles of droppings in their latrines.

You'll see bat droppings stuck to walls or on the ground under where bats roost and it's almost impossible to tell which species it comes from. You might even see bits of chewed up insects in the poo!

Hedgehog droppings are tube-shaped and often have shiny bits of insects inside, too.

MAMMALS

Wherever you live, you should be able to see and hear animals that become more active at night. These animals are known as 'nocturnal'. So get ready for a torchlight safari with this guide to some of the creatures you might find. And remember, you don't have to stay awake all night to spot interesting wildlife – dusk can be a great time to see nocturnal animals, too.

Mammals are animals that feed their babies with milk and usually have furry bodies. They come in all shapes and sizes, from humans to tiny little mice.

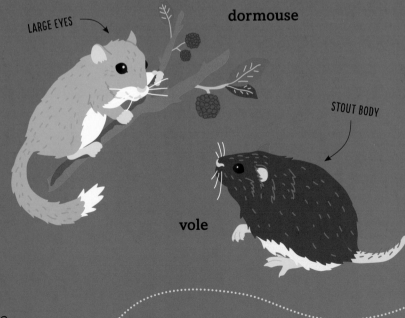

LARGE EYES

dormouse

STOUT BODY

vole

Some of the most common nocturnal
mammals are rodents such as mice, rats and voles.
They have large eyes, good hearing and long whiskers
to help them feel their way in the dark. Rodents also have
long tails which help them to balance, communicate and
control their body temperature.

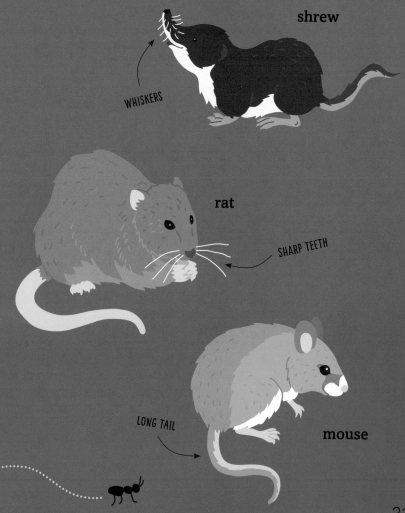

shrew

WHISKERS

rat

SHARP TEETH

LONG TAIL

mouse

You'll often see rabbits out and about at dusk, too. They usually stay close to their burrow and come out at dusk to eat grass and crops.

But don't get confused between rabbits and hares – brown hares are much larger than rabbits and have yellow eyes. They are most active at night and are usually alone.

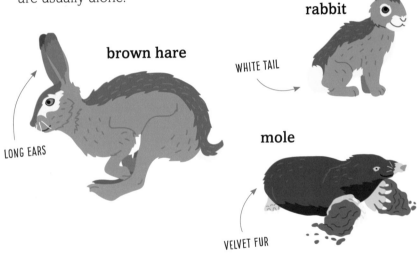

rabbit

brown hare

WHITE TAIL

LONG EARS

mole

VELVET FUR

Seeing a mole is very rare, but you might see their molehills while you're exploring. Moles spend most of their life underground, but they are surprisingly quick when they come above ground if they are flooded or they need to find a new place to live.

If you're lucky, you may spot a hedgehog in the wild. You will probably hear it snuffling around (and sometimes squealing!) before you catch sight of it.

hedgehog

SHARP SPINES

It's much harder for hedgehogs to find food during the winter, so they hibernate. This means they make a cosy nest of leaves and go into a deep sleep to save their energy. If they are scared, hedgehogs will roll up into a ball of sharp, spiky spines.

You might think hedgehogs are generally quiet animals, but you'll be surprised at how noisy they can be. Listen out for coughing, hissing and huffing noises, as well as screaming – and they even snore while they are snoozing!

FEEDING HEDGEHOGS

Hedgehogs mainly eat insects, but sometimes it can be hard for them to find food. Why don't you try feeding them, too?

1 Find a sheltered spot in your garden. To stop cats and foxes eating the food left out for hedgehogs, you will need to place a shallow dish of food inside a sturdy box to protect it.

2 Create a hedgehog-sized hole in the side of your box (about 13 cm square).

3 Add food to the shallow dish. The food needs to be hedgehog friendly – you could include:

- ★ Dried mealworms
- ★ Chopped nuts (unsalted)
- ★ Crushed cat biscuits
- ★ Cooked potatoes
- ★ Minced meat
- ★ Wet dog food (not fish or beef)
- ★ Chopped boiled eggs

Do not feed hedgehogs bread or milk as this will upset their stomachs!

4 Put a lid on top of the box and weigh it down so that another animal won't be able to tip it over.

5 Check to see when your dish is empty and, if you think you've had a night-time hedgehog visitor, refill the dish with food each evening.

6 Be careful, though – if you suspect that the food is being eaten by anything other than a hedgehog, stop putting out food!

MAMMALS

POINTY EARS

During breeding times, foxes make an alarming screaming noise as they are mating and protecting their territory. You'll hear them most during the winter, and they are much quieter in autumn.

fox

BUSHY TAIL

Foxes are mainly active during the night, when they come out to find food. You don't have to be in the countryside to see them – lots of foxes live in urban areas, too!

While you're on the hunt for foxes, look out carefully for these clues:

★ Reddish-brown tufts of fur on barbed wire fences and thorny hedges
★ Droppings that are smaller than dog droppings and pointed and twisted at one end. Make sure you don't touch them!
★ Footprints in soft ground or snow
★ Litter! Foxes often rip open bin bags during the night while they're trying to find food

CREAM 'BIB' MARKING

pine marten

Pine martens are also mainly active at dusk. They are about the same size as a domestic cat and have patches of cream fur on their throats, which makes them look like they are wearing a bib! They are very good at climbing trees because they have very sharp claws – and they can run fast on the ground, too!

During the day, badgers stay in their setts so you have a much better chance of seeing them by night. Badgers are very secretive animals, so approach the sett quietly and stay very still while you wait for them to appear. Badgers also have an excellent sense of smell, so don't use any strong-smelling soap before you go out.

badger

SHORT, FAT BODY

POWERFUL CLAWS

If you're on a nature walk through the woods or out in the countryside, you might hear badgers snorting, munching and coughing their way through the undergrowth. In fact, badgers have at least sixteen different calls, from growls to coos.

Although only found in Scotland now, the Scottish wildcat is most active at dawn or dusk. They look a lot like a domestic cat, but they have a much thicker, wider tail and black tiger-style stripes. You will usually find them alone in the wild.

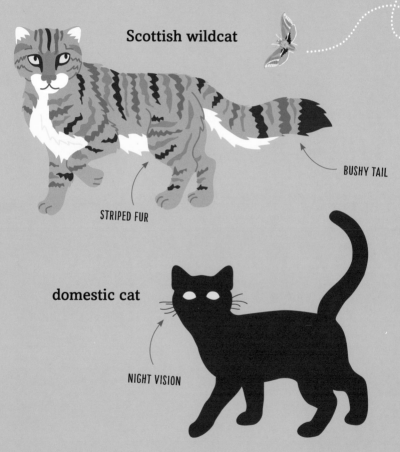

Scottish wildcat

BUSHY TAIL

STRIPED FUR

domestic cat

NIGHT VISION

All cats have something called tapetum in their eyeballs – this is a layer of light-reflecting cells which makes their eyes appear to glow in the dark.

MOTHS

Moths have pretty wings which are, in fact, just like butterflies' wings. They're made up of thousands of tiny overlapping scales but, unlike butterflies, moths only come out at night. There are over 2,500 species of moth in Britain, and they come in all different colours, shapes and sizes. Here are a few that you might see:

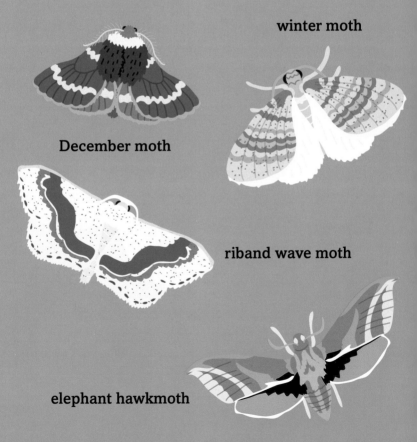

winter moth

December moth

riband wave moth

elephant hawkmoth

grey dagger moth

burnished brass moth

poplar hawkmoth

herald moth

blood-vein moth

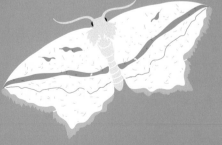

lime hawkmoth

brimstone moth

straw underwing moth

angle shades moth

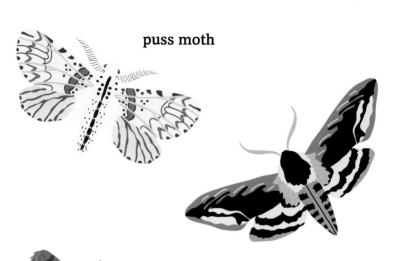

puss moth

privet hawkmoth

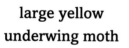

large yellow
underwing moth

cinnabar moth

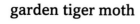

garden tiger moth

HOW TO ATTRACT MOTHS

There are two great ways you can attract moths to your garden. First, you can make your own trap by hanging up a white sheet and shining a bright torch onto it. The moths will begin to fly in and flutter around the light. Some will land on the sheet, so you can get a closer look.

 You can also attract moths by spreading sweet, sticky syrup around the trunk of a tree:

★ Mash up some overripe bananas and add brown sugar and treacle.

★ Pour on enough cola to make the mixture runny, but not so runny that it will drip.

★ Pour the mixture into a pan and gently heat it up (ask a grown-up to help you with this). Keep stirring until all the sugar has dissolved, then take it off the heat. Leave it to cool, stirring now and again.

★ Just before the sun sets, go outside and paint the mixture onto a tree trunk.

★ Once darkness falls, place red plastic over the beam of your torch and shine it over the syrup. Moths can't see red light, so if you keep quiet and still, you won't disturb any of the moths that are attracted to the tree.

NIGHT-TIME MINIBEASTS

As well as looking for moths fluttering through the sky, there's plenty of wildlife to be found down on the ground, too. Why don't you lift a log, turn a leaf or raise a plant to see what's hiding underneath?

You might find night-time minibeasts; these are simply small animals like insects or spiders. Most insects have three parts to their body: the head, the thorax (the part where an insect's six legs and wings grow from) and the abdomen (the rear part). Most insects live inside hard shells to protect them, because their bodies are soft and bendy, without a backbone.

Here are some more creepy-crawlies that you're likely to find out and about at night:

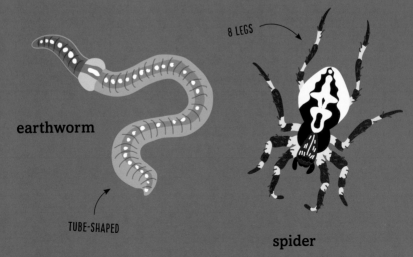

8 LEGS

earthworm

TUBE-SHAPED

spider

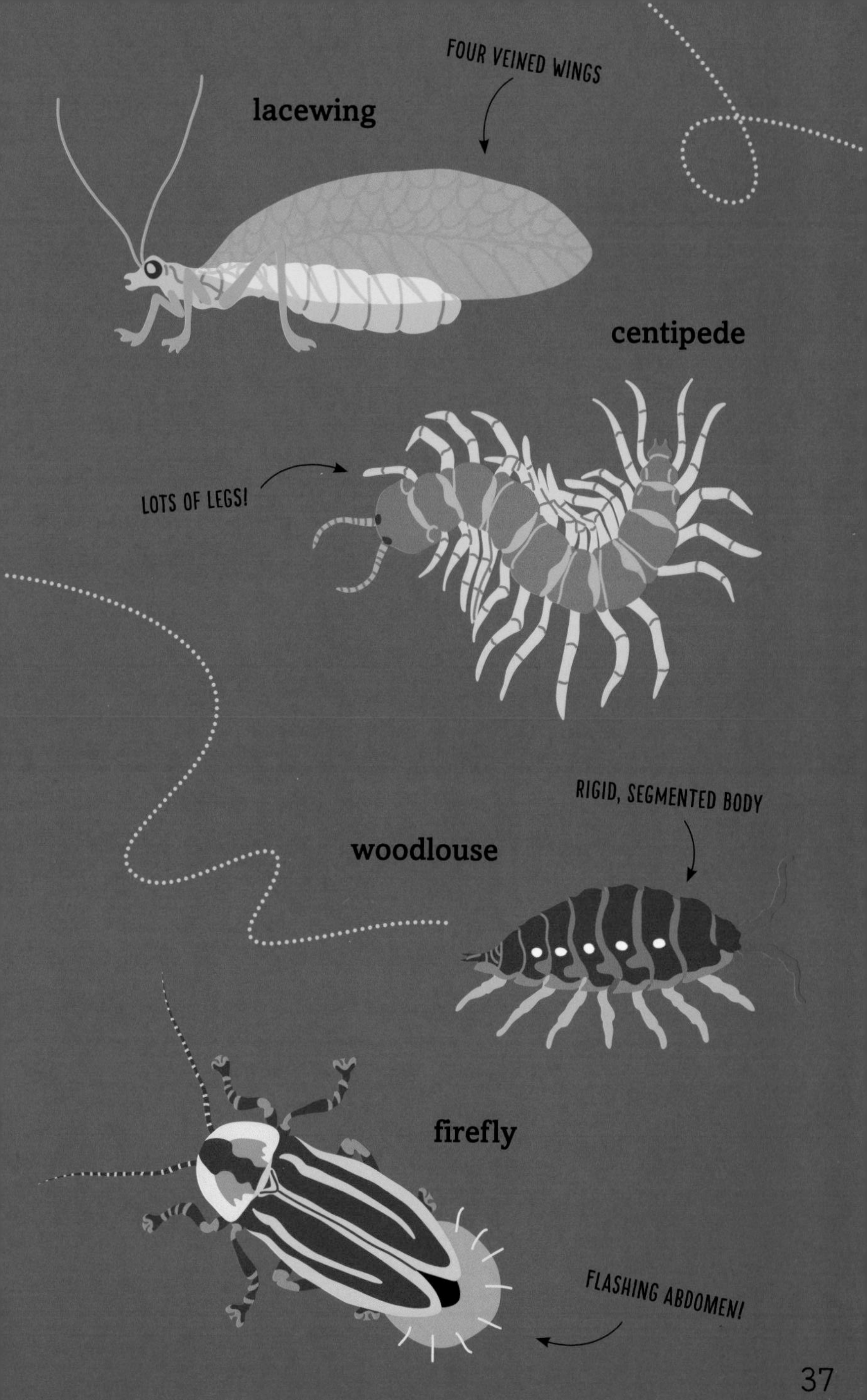

lacewing

FOUR VEINED WINGS

centipede

LOTS OF LEGS!

woodlouse

RIGID, SEGMENTED BODY

firefly

FLASHING ABDOMEN!

37

NIGHT-TIME MINIBEASTS

Look out for the silvery, slimy trail of slugs and snails in the dark. They come out at night so they won't get eaten by hungry birds during the daytime. You might find them clustered in cracks in rockeries, on walls, behind plants like ivy, under logs or in old flowerpots.

slug

SLIMY TRAIL

LARGE THIGHS

cricket

snail

HARD SHELL

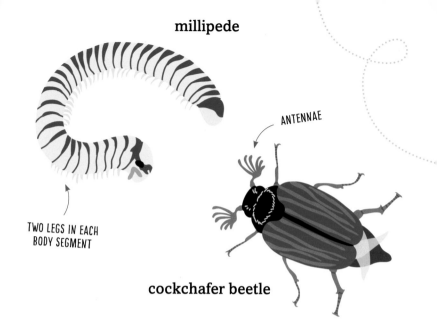

millipede

ANTENNAE

TWO LEGS IN EACH
BODY SEGMENT

cockchafer beetle

If you're near a pond, you might also find insects such as
water boatmen and pond skaters.

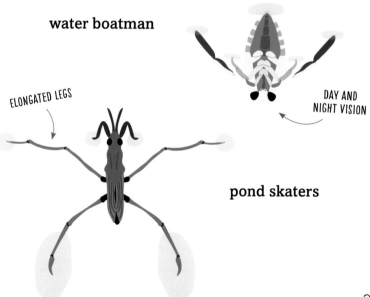

water boatman

ELONGATED LEGS

DAY AND
NIGHT VISION

pond skaters

MAKING A CREEPY-CRAWLY HOUSE

During the winter, you can help minibeasts by making them a cosy habitat with lots of hidey-holes.

1 Find a level spot of firm ground in your garden.

2 Start to build the basic structure by placing bricks on the ground and then stacking up crates, palettes or old planks of wood.

3 Fill in all the gaps to create lots of cosy nooks and crannies for bugs to move into. You could use:

- ★ Loose bark and dead wood
- ★ Dry leaves
- ★ Straw
- ★ Twigs
- ★ Moss
- ★ Feathers
- ★ Fir cones

BATS

Bats are small, furry mammals that hang upside down to nest during the day and are very active at night. There's a good chance you will see them darting through the night sky looking for insects while you're exploring. Look out for them flying around streetlights in towns and cities – they can be very small and very fast! Calm, humid evenings are best for bat-watching as bats don't fly about if it's windy or rainy.

Some bats are small enough to fit in the palm of your hand and weigh the same as a lump of sugar!

There are lots of species in Britain; here are some that you might find in the wild:

pipistrelle bat

TINY FEET WITH
FIVE TOES AND CLAWS

The long-eared bat has huge powerful ears which they use to find their way and avoid obstacles when they're flying.

VERY LARGE EARS

long-eared bat

LONG-EARED BAT AT CORRECT SCALE

The barbastelle bat is medium-sized and has a face shaped like a pug!

barbastelle bat

PUG NOSE

The noctule bat is one of Britain's largest bats (although you could still fit it in the palm of your hand!) and it sometimes comes out in the daytime.

DELICATE WINGS

noctule bat

The Daubenton's bat is known as the 'water bat' because it likes to fly low over water to pick up insects.

FLUFFY, FURRY BODY

Daubenton's bat

The whiskered bat has shaggy fur and long hairs around its mouth.

whiskered bat

WHISKERS

OWLS

Most owls are nocturnal and you'll often be able to hear one before you see it. Owls can often be found in woodland, parks and gardens, but you can catch sight of them flying through the sky as they search for their prey.

Keep your eyes peeled for the barn owl's heart-shaped face, pale brown back and wings, and pure white underparts.

barn owl

HEART-SHAPED FACE

The most famous night-time animal noise is probably the 'twit twoo' of owls, but actually there are lots of different species of owl and each makes a different sound. Listen out for the long eerie shriek of the barn owl, heard as it glides over a meadow.

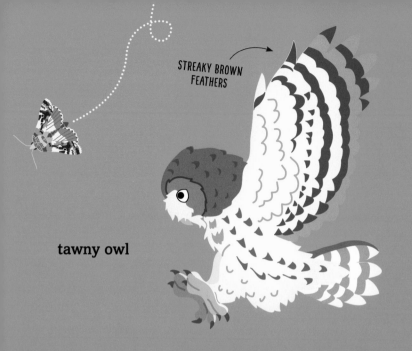

STREAKY BROWN FEATHERS

tawny owl

Tawny owls are our most common type of owl and they are about the same size as a pigeon. They have a ring of dark feathers around their faces surrounding their dark eyes.

The tawny owl makes the classic 'twit twoo' sound, although they go silent during June and July. Female owls make the 'twit' sound and males answer with a 'twoo', so when you hear 'twit twoo', it is actually two owls chatting!

OWLS

You're likely to find short-eared owls out in open countryside rather than in woodland. Look out for them flying overhead as they hunt for mice, voles and shrews in the field below.

short-eared owl

HOOKED BEAK

Snowy owls are very rare, but if you're in Scotland you might just catch sight of one. They are almost all pure white so they stand out beautifully against the night sky!

snowy owl

YELLOW EYES

48

Long-eared owls are very shy and you'll have to look very hard to find one. They stay hidden because the colour of their feathers helps them to blend into the tree trunks. This is called camouflage.

BLACK EAR TUFTS

long-eared owl

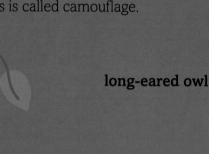

Little owls are tiny and you'll usually find them perching on a tree branch, telegraph pole or rock. Little owls make a sharp 'kiew kiew kiew' sound, as well as a single 'woop' call.

little owl

SMALL, PLUMP BODY

Apart from owls, there are a few other nocturnal birds, which you might be lucky enough to hear during the spring and summer months.

PLAIN BROWN FEATHERS

nightingale

It's much easier to hear a nightingale than to see one, but you'll only be able to hear it between April and June. It does sing during the day, but is more commonly heard after dark. Its song is very musical with lots of high and low notes.

Nightingales are very shy, secretive birds and they're very difficult to see because they are plain brown and they like nothing better than hiding in the middle of a dense bush.

Although they are nocturnal, you might also see nightjars as they hunt for moths and other large flying insects on heathland during dusk and dawn. They have mottled grey and brown feathers which means they can stay well hidden in the trees during the daytime.

The nightjar has a bizarre purring song and can sometimes purr for five minutes without a break!

nightjar

LONG, POINTED WINGS

AMPHIBIANS

Night-time is also the perfect time to go looking for amphibians like frogs, toads and newts. They have smooth skin with no fur or scales and their skin dries out in bright sunlight. This means they usually come out of their hiding places at night, when the temperature is cooler and they won't be exposed to the sun.

If you're on a nature walk near a pond or marsh (especially after it's been raining), you might be able to hear the sound of frogs and toads. The best time of year is between January and March because it rains a lot and amphibians will be making lots of noise as they try to find a mate.

Newts are attracted to light, so if you shine your torch on the surface of the pond and quietly wait, you might just spot one.

Look out for these amphibians while you're exploring:

WARTY SKIN

common toad

common frog

WEBBED FEET

smooth newt

ORANGE BELLY

ANIMALS THAT GLOW

Some animals are much easier to see at night because they actually make light themselves. This is called bioluminescence. If you're near grassland, look out for tiny pinpricks of light – this might be a firefly! This type of beetle usually hides away during the daytime, but during the night the female crawls to the tops of tall blades of grass and starts to glow in order to attract the male.

The best place to look for fireflies is in an area with lots of trees and plants, particularly in hidden, dark places close to the ground. It also helps if there's a pond, river or lake nearby. You are most likely to see them at the end of spring and summer, but they're not always easy to find!

As well as fireflies, all sorts of other animals can glow in the dark – insects, fish, spiders and worms! In deep, dark waters some fish and squid glow in the dark and use their lights to attract food. It also helps them to see where they are going.

fireflies

There are nocturnal animals all over the world – not just in the UK. In fact, there are thousands of creatures that wait for darkness to fall before coming out to hunt for food.

Here are just a few of the wide range of night-loving animals from around the world:

wolf

STRONG JAW

Wild dogs like wolves, coyotes and jackals hunt at night. Much like foxes, they use their large, sensitive noses to help them sniff out their prey. Their sense of smell is fifty times better than a human's!

Raccoons have excellent eyesight – and very sensitive fingertips, too. They use their long fingers to scavenge for food.

raccoon

BLACK MASK MARKING

AROUND THE WORLD

Mammals that have pouches, like kangaroos, koalas and Tasmanian devils, are called marsupials, and they are mostly nocturnal. Koalas spend all day sleeping and all night eating eucalyptus leaves.

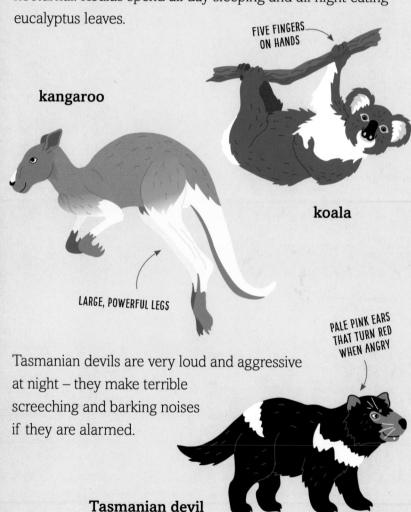

FIVE FINGERS ON HANDS

kangaroo

koala

LARGE, POWERFUL LEGS

Tasmanian devils are very loud and aggressive at night – they make terrible screeching and barking noises if they are alarmed.

PALE PINK EARS THAT TURN RED WHEN ANGRY

Tasmanian devil

Tarsiers are strange-looking nocturnal creatures that live in tropical rainforests. They have enormous eyes which help them to hunt for insects at night.

LONG FINGERS
AND TOES

tarsier

EXCELLENT
HEARING

Bushbabies also have huge eyes so they can see well in the dark. During the day, they huddle together in hollow trees, but by night, they run around in the branches looking for food.

bushbaby

gecko

In hot countries, reptiles often wait until the sun's gone down so that it's much cooler and their delicate skin isn't damaged by the bright sun. They have large eyes, which help them to see in the dark.

TOE PADS TO HELP
CLIMB WALLS

AROUND THE WORLD

Since many insects are active by night, so are the mammals that hunt them, including aardvarks, armadillos and pangolins.

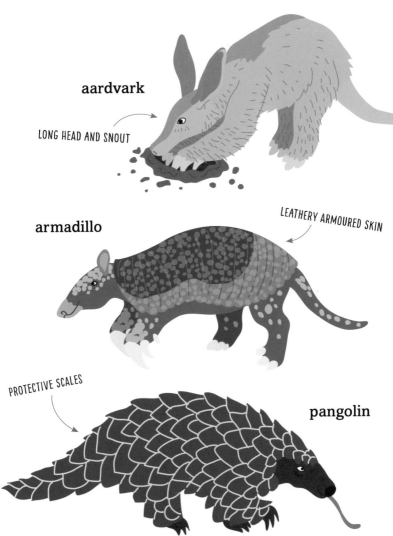

aardvark

LONG HEAD AND SNOUT

armadillo

LEATHERY ARMOURED SKIN

PROTECTIVE SCALES

pangolin

PLANTS

NIGHT-TIME FLOWERS

When you're outside in the dark, you might also notice the strong scent of flowers. That's because many plants actually do pump out more perfume after the sun has gone down. You might even say that some of these flowers are semi-nocturnal!

As well as having a strong scent, many of the flowers are pale or white, so that they are easier for insects to see against the darkness. Not only are they beautiful as they reflect the moonlight, but a garden full of night-scented flowers also attracts lots of night-time wildlife, such as moths and bats.

Here is a list of flowers that are magnets for moths and will help turn your garden into a night garden:

buddleia

jasmine

eryngium giganteum

nicotiana

night phlox

honeysuckle

wisteria

verbena

globe artichoke

caryopteris

hebe

evening primrose

The evening primrose's petals stay closed during the daytime, and uncurl amazingly rapidly at dusk!

THE NIGHT SKY

It's not just wildlife that's interesting at night. If you look up into the night sky, you'll be amazed at what's out there!

THE MOON

It's almost impossible not to notice the moon while you're exploring the night-time. But the moon isn't always easy to see. This is because it's constantly moving around our planet, and as it moves, we can see different parts of it lit up by the reflected light of the sun. The moon also helps to control sea levels and tides, because of its 'gravitational pull'.

Sometimes finding the moon isn't easy at all – it can be too cloudy or the moon might be hiding behind a building or hill. If you live in a city, it's best to go to an area where you can see a good portion of the sky.

On a clear night, you can try and work out which phase of its monthly cycle the moon is in. You could start keeping a moon diary and track the moon for a month. Each night you can draw what shape you see to record your very own moon cycle.

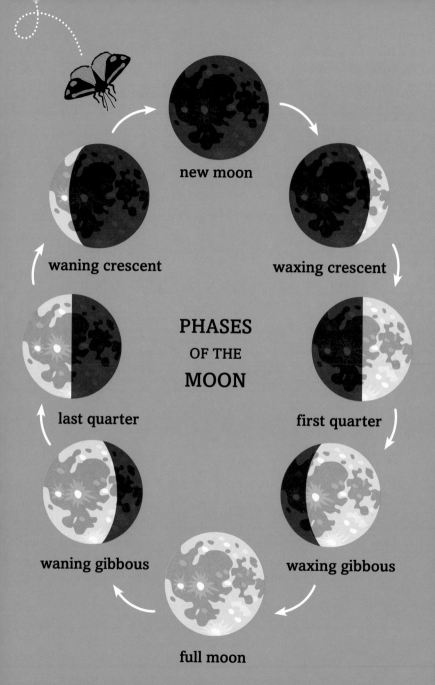

new moon

waxing crescent

waning crescent

PHASES
OF THE
MOON

first quarter

last quarter

waxing gibbous

waning gibbous

full moon

65

STARGAZING

There's so much more than the moon in the night sky. As soon as your eyes have got used to the darkness, you'll start to notice thousands of tiny, twinkling stars – and even the odd planet!

Groups of stars are called constellations and you can use star maps to help you find the different star shapes. It can be tricky, so ask a grown-up to help you, too. And it's even better if you have a telescope, so you can really get a closer look. Some constellations look like animals or objects, so they can be easier to spot and remember.

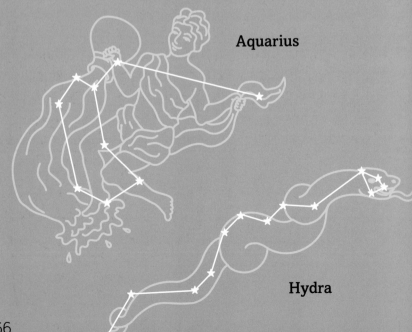

Aquarius

Hydra

Cancer

Leo

Orion

Aries

67

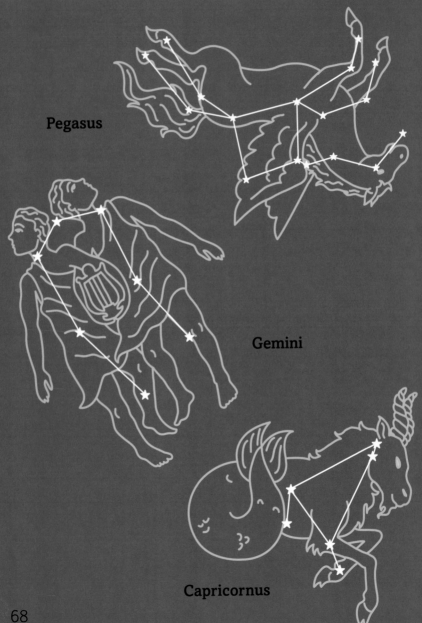

Pegasus

Gemini

Capricornus

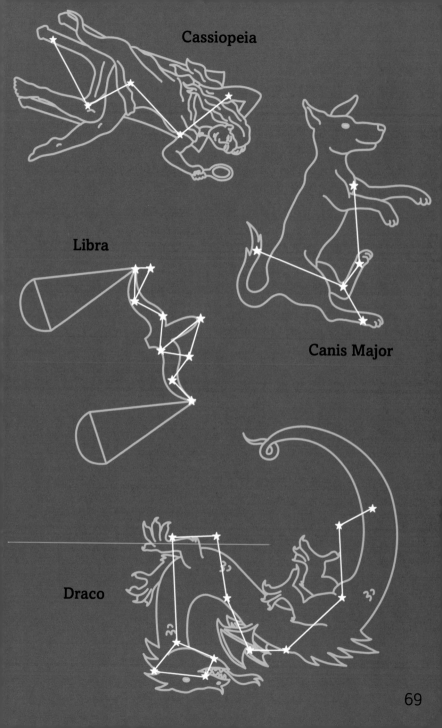

Cassiopeia

Libra

Canis Major

Draco

69

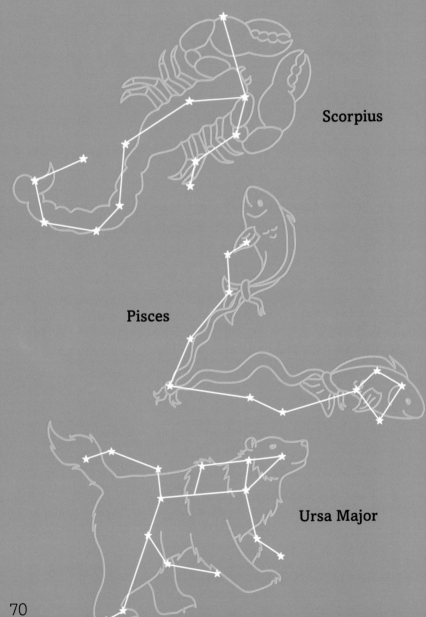

Scorpius

Pisces

Ursa Major

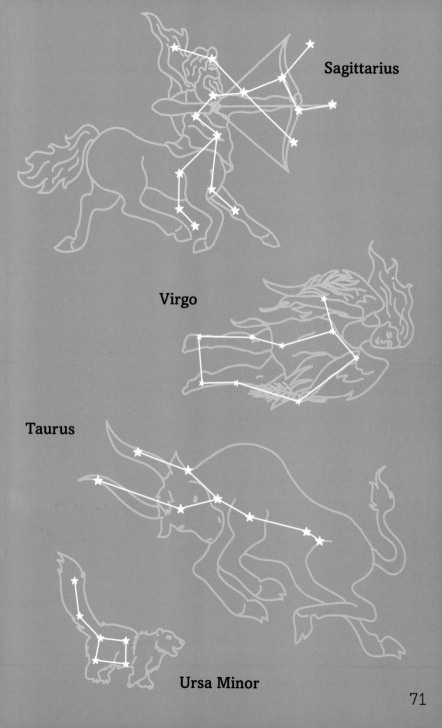

Sagittarius

Virgo

Taurus

Ursa Minor

71

NIGHT-TIME ACTIVITIES

SENSORY MAP

We all have five senses which work together to give us a clear picture of the things around us. These are sight, smell, sound, touch and taste. If one sense isn't working, then the other senses will take over or become stronger to make up for the missing sense. When it's dark outside, you can't see as well as in the daytime, so the other four senses become stronger to make up for it.

One fun activity to try in the dark is creating a map of all the things you notice with all of your senses. Head out on a walk you know well and take a piece of paper and a pencil with you. As you're walking, make a note of any special sounds, smells or textures that you experience. Then go back in the daytime and see if you can follow your map. Do you notice the same things when it's light outside?

It's the same for animals, too! Animals that come out at night often have a stronger sense of smell because it's harder for them to see. So, try to avoid smelling strongly of perfume or going out just after you've had a bubble bath – the animals will smell you coming a mile off!

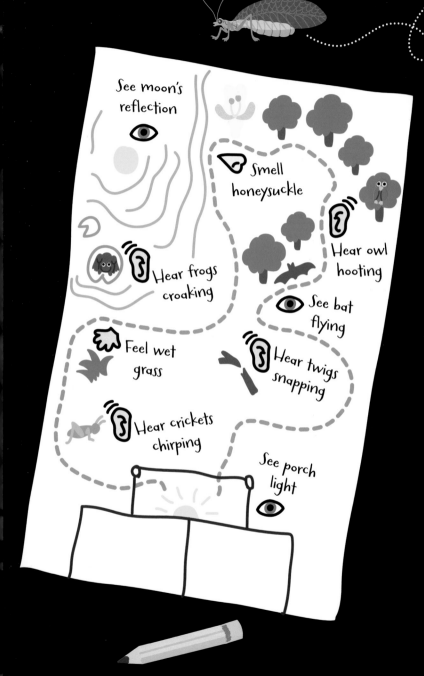

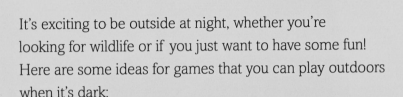

NIGHT-TIME GAMES

It's exciting to be outside at night, whether you're looking for wildlife or if you just want to have some fun! Here are some ideas for games that you can play outdoors when it's dark:

 1 Hide-and-seek

Hiding in the dark means you can find many more great hiding places. The seeker can use their torch to find the players that are hiding.

 2 Sardines

This is a bit like hide-and-seek, but only one person hides while the rest of the players shut their eyes and count to twenty. Everyone splits up to look for the hider. Once the hider is found, each person must hide together in the same hiding spot, until there's only one person left searching.

 3 Storytelling

Night-time is the perfect opportunity to use your imagination and tell stories – try telling funny, true or even scary stories! Take it in turns to tell your own tales, or make them up with your friends. Someone should start off the story, then the next person adds a twist, and so on.

4   Grandma's footsteps

One player is chosen to be 'Grandma' and stands at the opposite end of the garden from the other players, facing away from them. The other players try to sneak up on 'Grandma' without being heard. If she hears footsteps, she shines her torch at the culprit and they go back to the start. The first person to touch 'Grandma' on the shoulder without being caught is the winner.

5   Glow-in-the-dark paint

Painting is messy fun whenever and wherever you do it, but with glow-in-the-dark paints, it can be lots of fun to paint outside at night. You could paint a picture of the moon and stars or even some of the creatures that you might have found on your nature walk.

6   Bat and moth game

For this game you need a group of people to be standing in a circle. These players are called 'trees'. Standing inside the circle one person is chosen to be the bat and blindfolded and another person is the moth. The bat calls out 'bat, bat, bat' and the moth echoes by saying 'moth' whenever the bat calls. The moth must dodge the bat but stay within the circle, and the bats need to keep calling to try and catch them. The trees can call out 'tree' if anyone is in danger of bumping into them. You can play with more moths to make it trickier for the bat!

NIGHT EXPLORER QUIZ

1 **What is dusk?**
a) Fox droppings
b) The period between light and darkness at the end of each day
c) The pattern on a moth's wings

2 **Which of these mammals is not nocturnal?**
a) Vole
b) Badger
c) Squirrel

3 **What does this word say**
— — — • — — • — • • ?
a) Owl
b) Fox
c) Cat

4 **What does a hedgehog do if it's scared?**
a) Roll up into a ball
b) Roll on its back and lie still
c) Run away

5 **Which one of these foods should you feed hedgehogs?**
a) Bread
b) Mealworms
c) Milk

6 **What does tapetum do?**
a) Marks an animal's territory
b) Attracts moths to a white sheet
c) Makes cats' eyes glow in the dark

7 **Which of these is not a type of moth?**
a) Lime hawkmoth
b) Rhinoceros hawkmoth
c) Elephant hawkmoth

8 **What are moths attracted to?**
a) Light
b) Heat
c) Water

12) c 13) b 14) c 15) b

76

9 How many legs does an insect have?

a) Four
b) Six
c) Eight

10 What do bats eat?

a) Bread
b) Insects
c) Leaves

11 Which is the most common type of owl in the UK?

a) Tawny owl
b) Snowy owl
c) Long-eared owl

12 Which nocturnal bird sometimes makes a bizarre purring sound?

a) Barn owl
b) Nightingale
c) Nightjar

13 Which plant has petals that uncurl at night?

a) Buddleia
b) Evening primrose
c) Honeysuckle

14 Which of these is not a phase of the moon?

a) Waxing gibbous
b) Waning crescent
c) Third quarter

15 What are groups of stars called?

a) Starshapes
b) Constellations
c) Telescopes

Amphibian
A cold-blooded animal with a skeleton that spends part of its life in water and part on land, such as frogs and toads.

Breeding
Producing young animals.

Camouflage
Markings which help an animal to blend into their surroundings.

Compass
A tool with a magnetic needle used for showing direction.

Constellation
Groups of bright stars forming patterns in the sky.

Droppings
Animal poo.

Dusk
The time of day before night.

Gravity
A force which pulls two objects toward each other.

Habitat
A particular type of place where a group of animals or plants lives, such as mountains or woodland.

Hibernate
To sleep through winter in a den or burrow to save energy.

Invertebrate
A creature without a backbone, such as insects and worms.

Latrine
A toilet used by a group of animals.

Mammal
A warm-blooded animal with a skeleton and fur on its skin. Mammal mothers produce milk to feed their babies.

Morse code
A code where letters of the alphabet and numbers are represented by dots and dashes, or by short and long flashes of light or sound.

Nocturnal
Active at night.

Pellet
The solid waste of particular animals, e.g. rabbits and hares.

Predator
An animal that hunts other animals for food.

Prey
An animal hunted by other animals for food.

Rodent
A small mammal with long front teeth for gnawing.

Sett
A badger family's underground home.

Species
A particular kind of animal.

Territory
An area that is marked and defended by a particular type of animal.

Tracks
Footprints or an animal pathway.

Urban
Relating to a town or a city.

Vertebrate
An animal with a backbone: mammals, birds, reptiles, amphibians and fishes.

INDEX